The Empowered Advocate

Change the World
AND
Love What You Do

By Pamela Jacobs, J.D.

The Empowered Advocate

By Pamela Jacobs, J.D.

"I've learned that people will forget what you said, people will forget what you did, but people will never forget how you made them feel." ~

Dr. Maya Angelou

If you are reading these pages, you are one of the thousands of dedicated women and men who have chosen to work in one of the most difficult – and most fulfilling— professions.

You are an advocate.

You meet people at what is often the lowest point in their lives. You see the invisible and mend the broken. You give people hope and help them find their voice. And as someone who was once voiceless, I want first to say, from the depth of my heart: Thank you.

This book is dedicated to you. My hope is that it will remind you that you are truly transforming lives and constantly changing the world. I hope it will not only give you tools to utilize when working to empower survivors, but will also help you to empower yourself.

But, I should also warn you: The book you are holding is not just informative, it will also force you to be introspective. I have asked you to do some work, and self-reflection. Throughout these pages, you will see prompts asking you to write for two minutes. These exercises are for *you*, to help you uncover hidden blocks and rediscover your passion.

I have asked you to set a timer because:

1. I believe the most real, authentic responses come out in the first few moments of writing; and

2. I know you are incredibly busy.

Please try to be completely open and honest in your responses. I believe you will be intrigued by your answers – and how much you already know!

Your work is important. You are important. I am so grateful you have chosen this book, and that you are choosing you – because YOU matter.

Chapter One

Remembering Why We Do What We Do

If you've been in this work for more than a week, you've probably heard, "How do you do it? It must be so depressing/hard/sucky/life-draining," or something to that effect. And let's be honest – it can be. This *is* hard work. And it can absolutely drain and depress us– if we let it.

After all, we are faced with unspeakable horrors every day. We see the things most people would rather ignore. We know all too well that multiple women are murdered every day by current or former partners.

We know that someone chooses to commit a rape in the United States every 90 seconds. We know at least one in three girls and one in six boys under the age of 18 will be sexually abused. We know that awful, violent things happen every day. We know, because we see it.

Now, I have a question for you ... Did you just read through that entire horrifying list with absolutely no reaction? No goosebumps, no shock and horror, no pit in your stomach, no tears? If so, you are in trouble, my friend.

We have become so accustom to these facts that they no longer shock us. You probably read through that list thinking, "Tell me something I don't know, lady."

Now, imagine you are new to this work. Imagine you've never heard of domestic or sexual violence. Imagine you live in a happy, joyful world where these things don't exist – or, at least, where they are frequently ignored. Put on those rose-colored glasses for a moment, and read that list again.

- Multiple women are *murdered* every day by current or former partners.
- Someone chooses to commit a *rape* every 90 seconds.
- At least one in three girls and one in six boys under the age of 18 will be *sexually abused*.

These facts *should* shock us – because they're absolutely shocking! You may be wondering why I'm starting this book by reminding you of all the terrible, frightful things in the world. It probably doesn't make you feel terribly empowered, right? Well, I'm getting all the awful stuff out up front, because then we can move on.

I'm not a fan of statistics. I think they do very little to help convey our message, and definitely don't help us empower anyone. It's hard for people to connect with numbers. So, this is probably the last time you'll read depressing numbers in this book. You're welcome.

But, I mention these horrific facts because it's important to remember *why* we do this work. We have become so desensitized to these horrors that they no longer scare or shock us. We can listen to a woman recount horrific abuse and not even flinch. In some ways, that is a necessary part of doing this work well – and not losing our minds. But, it's important that we don't, in the process, lose our humanity.

Do you remember the *first time* someone shared a painful story of abuse with you? Do you remember that rock in the pit of your stomach, and the tingle that ran up your spine? Do you remember that incredible urge you felt to do something – *anything!* – to help that person? Of course you do. That urge is the reason why any of us stay in this work past our first week.

We used to be shocked and mortified at these numbers, and especially at the stories. But then, we became overworked and frustrated. Most of all, we grew to be exhausted. And now, I hear from advocates all the time who say things such as, "I've heard it all. Nothing shocks me anymore."

If a survivor told you that nothing her abusive partner did shocked or bothered her anymore, you'd probably think she was in denial, or suffering the effects of trauma, right?

Hmmmm......I wonder if we might be, as well?

Throughout these pages, we're going to talk about ways to improve your (and our collective) response to survivors. But first, take a few minutes to recall *why* you got involved in this work, and why you decided to stick around.

Set a timer and write for two minutes.

_____

_____

_____

_____

_____

_____

Did you write words and phrases like "help," change the world," or "make a difference"? I want you to remember that.

The next time you find yourself frustrated with a survivor who just isn't "getting it" (more on that later) or feeling discouraged by the abundance of work and scarcity of resources, I want you to come back to this page and read your *WHY*. Really let your *reason* for doing this work become part of who you are. Let it propel you forward, and be your safety net for support when you are most overwhelmed.

And if you reach a point when you can't remember your why, or no longer feel motivated by it, it may be time for a change. Stay tuned for more on that soon.

Chapter Two

Unpacking Our Own Stuff

Before we can ever truly be successful at helping anyone else heal from trauma, we must begin the work of healing from our own. I say "begin" the work, not "do" the work, because I believe healing is never fully *done*. It's a continual process, and a journey toward, not *getting over* trauma, but becoming continually more aware and more adept at *responding* to it.

For anyone reading this who is a trained trauma counselor or neuroscientist, the following non-scientific analogy may make you cringe. Please, bear with me.

I tend to think of trauma as being stored in boxes in our brains. Often, at the time of a traumatic experience, our brains seal up the box-of-trauma, mostly to protect us. The phenomenal and brilliant Dr. Rebecca Campbell[1] refers to trauma memories as post-it notes scattered on a messy desk – the memories are there, but they're often incredibly difficult to locate. That's probably a much better analogy. But, since I got started with my boxes, let's keep going…

So, the boxes are sealed up. This is why our memories of trauma are often fragmented, out of order, or seem to not make any sense. This is also why people who are not trained in trauma often mistakenly accuse trauma survivors (especially sexual assault survivors) of lying. They mistake the lack of chronological memories as a sign of fabrication, instead of recognizing them as a symptom of trauma.[2]

We often go about our lives happily (or at least quasi-happy) for quite some time – years even – with those traumatic memories and feelings securely tucked away in those boxes. The problem, however, is that the boxes aren't taped shut very well. Our brain apparently doesn't use heavy-duty duct tape. So, someday, something will likely happen to make pop them open.

Like some of you, I have moved around a lot in my life – both due to my history of childhood abuse and my previous marriage to a member of the military. So, I have often been surrounded by many (actual) boxes. And I have also tried to avoid unpacking for as long as I possibly could – because unpacking boxes is not fun, it's hard work. I have also had many unpacked trauma boxes, for the same reasons. Unpacking trauma is, certainly, not fun.

And, just like my household boxes, I have tried to ignore those pesky trauma boxes, too. Unlike household goods, you can't just throw those annoying boxes in the garage, label them as "miscellaneous" and pretend the movers lost them. I mean, hypothetically, of course.

Trauma boxes won't just sit in the corner quietly. They won't just wait until your next move and keep sitting quietly, until someone really does forget them. Eventually, something will happen, and those boxes *will* pop open. Then, the contents will be screaming, demanding to be acknowledged and appropriately stored and dealt with.

The "something" that comes along may be someone passing by wearing the same cologne as someone who hurt you in the past. It may be a feeling of helplessness or conflict in a close relationship. It could be a break-up that brings up feelings of abandonment or vulnerability. These "somethings" are triggers. They are the box cutters that slice open the flimsy tape and leave your trauma box open

and exposed, its contents demanding to be seen.

For me, one of my biggest triggers – the box cutter – was

the smell of motor oil. I was sexually abused my entire

childhood by my step-grandfather, who was a mechanic.

So, any time I would go to a shop to get my car worked on,

I would feel sick to my stomach and immediately anxious.

(This is a problem since, as a non-profit advocate, I have

typically driven cars in need of frequent repair). After

leaving the shop, I would often have nightmares for days.

And I would be hyper-vigilant (over-protective) with my

daughter – even more than usual.

For years, I had no idea what was causing these feelings.

Since I didn't recognize the trigger, my trauma box kept

popping open, then hastily repacking itself, then popping

open again. Each time, the trigger caused the same results. And each time, I ignored the box. Until one day, I realized that maybe I didn't just dislike mechanics – maybe this was actually caused by some memories I hadn't recognized.

As soon as I became *aware* of the trigger, I took back control of it. Instead of being surprised and thrown off by the box popping open, I took charge of when it happened. I *chose* to open it.

I unpacked the box.

The unpacking process brought back some difficult and painful memories. But, the sense of control over the process was freeing and empowering. I was now holding that box cutter securely in my hand.

Triggers may never completely go away, but they can lose their power over us. So now, when I take my car to the shop, I know that I may not like the smell. I am prepared. And if my stomach starts to hurt, I know that it is temporary and it will pass. I know that I am safely in the present moment, not back in my childhood. I no longer have nightmares after going to the mechanic, and I am no longer hyper-vigilant. I am *aware*. The box no longer pops open without my knowledge. I open it myself, examine the contents, and put them away.

For many of us, the triggers come along in the form of a survivor whose story is just a bit too close to our own, or who responded in a similar way or reminds of us something in our past. Or it may even be a survivor who is very different than us and had a very different reaction than we did. Triggers are often like that – sometimes they don't always make sense.

In my first year as an advocate, I learned how powerful triggers can be in this work. It was a Saturday night and I was on call. Which, at that ancient time, meant I had the responsibility of carrying the gigantic on-call phone – since many of us did not have our own cell phones back then (and we rode T-Rexes to work).

At about 3am, the phone rang: a call from the hospital. (Isn't it always at 3am?). A 15-year-old girl had come to the Emergency Room for a forensic exam after being raped by a man at a county fair. I jumped out of bed and threw on my sweats and t-shirt (which I had laid out in preparation for a call). Since I had been unable to locate childcare for my on-call weekend, my then infant daughter came to the hospital with me. (I don't recommend this, by the way).

Thankfully, a very sweet nurse who I had gotten to know well offered to watch my daughter while I visited with the survivor.

As I walked into the room, I was hit with the angry voices of the survivor's family members, yelling at her and accusing her of lying. "You just made this all up so you could sleep with another [racial slur]." I later learned that the perpetrator was an African American man. The survivor, who was white, had previously dated African American young men from school, which enraged her apparently bigoted family. Her grandmother, who was her guardian and primary caretaker, was particularly upset, yelling vile and hurtful comments.

I took a deep breath and remembered why I was there: to support the survivor. I introduced myself and asked if I could please have a moment alone with her. I stayed at the hospital with her until 8am – giving me just enough time to get home, shower, get my baby girl to daycare, and get to work by 9am.

As soon as I walked in the office, I felt physically ill, and spent most of the morning in the bathroom throwing up. Of course, exhaustion and the trauma of being in the ER would be explanation enough. But, it was far more than that – I had been triggered.

The scene at the hospital brought back memories and feelings of my own grandmother, who raised me, yelling at me and calling me a liar when I, also at the age of 15, told her that her husband had sexually abused me. And the racial slurs being hurled by the survivor's family brought back painful memories of my own family accusing me of lying just so I could move out and sneak around with my "black friends."

I grew up in a very diverse area and had a very diverse group of friends, including many interracial couples. And many of my closest friends were African American. Of course, the family's slurs were made even more painful because, my own daughter, is multi-ethnic – and was, unfortunately, at the hospital with me.

It was all too much. The trauma box was bursting open faster than I could possibly process the contents. And my body reacted strongly. But, I wasn't aware enough at the time of my trauma, or my own body, so I didn't realize what was happening. Instead, I rationalized that the survivor just had a terrible, evil family, and she needed me to save her. (Hint: The savior urge is *almost always* a sign of unpacked trauma).

So, I did what any unaware and traumatized advocate would do: I became overly involved and crossed all kinds of boundaries. I started giving her rides to work, gave her my personal phone number to reach me *any* time, and started plotting ways to get her out of her evil grandmother's house.

As you might imagine, this did not work out well. The survivor needed far more support than I, on my own, could provide. And the combination of trying to meet all of her needs, while simultaneously ignoring my own, became exhausting and frustrating. I eventually had to back away, set better boundaries, and figure out why I was so emotionally impacted by her story.

It took many years, but I eventually figured it out. And again, simply being aware is all it takes to reclaim power over your triggers. And that power is what can help you not only be healthier for yourself, but also for every survivor you serve.

What are your triggers? Are you aware of them yet? If not, start to keep track of when you feel anxious, unsafe, afraid, or just uneasy. In that moment, is something happening that could be a trigger for you?

Remember, triggers can happen even if you are not a survivor of sexual assault or domestic violence. Other forms of trauma –like a car accident, serious illness, or a natural disaster – can also leave trauma boxes that are ready and waiting to pop open. You may also be storing trauma boxes from someone else's trauma. We're seeing this a lot in military spouses, who are now carrying not only their own trauma, but also the trauma of their combat veteran spouse.

Start by recognizing when you feel triggered, then you can trace back to *what* is being triggered – and unpack the box.

If you are aware of your triggers, set a two-minute timer and write about them here. If you are not, use this space to write any time you feel yourself being triggered, and see if you can identify the root of that feeling—the trauma box.

_____

_____

_____

Chapter Three

Seeing Clearly

Picture this: You're sitting in your office (cubicle, yurt, whatever) and a woman calls or walks in and starts screaming at you. She's angry that the perpetrator was (or wasn't) arrested, she's angry that she has to miss work, she's angry that she can't reach the prosecutor, she's just freaking ANGRY – and right now, she's angry *at you*.

Has that ever happened to you? If not, welcome to advocacy. I hope you're enjoying your first week. Re-read this section in about a month.

Seriously, anyone who has been in this work for a while has been yelled at. We are dealing with trauma. And frankly, we serve people who have every right to be pissed off. We know that, but it doesn't help us in the moment when we're being screamed at. So, what do we do?

Let them be angry.

If the survivor is standing in your office, you can simply ask that she have a seat, and then sit beside her. Let her know that it is important to you that you both feel safe. Tell her that she has every right to be angry. Encourage her to let it out.

When we give someone permission to feel whatever they feel, they can better process that emotion and get to what they're really feeling. Anger is rarely the true emotion. Anger is a secondary emotion, and is usually masking something much more difficult to express. As Liza Palmer said, "Angry is just sad's bodyguard." It may also be fear's bodyguard or grief's bodyguard. Emotions that are too scary or vulnerable to truly process and display often come out masked as anger.

But any type of emotion, when given the chance to be expressed, can pass quickly. In fact, you'll likely have this same person crying within a few minutes.

Some of you may be thinking that it's not survivors' behavior that bothers you. You've done this work for a while and have been to a dozen trauma-informed trainings – thank you very much. But, your frustration is with all the *other assholes* you have to deal with. Believe me, I get it.

What about that law enforcement officer who yells at victims? Or the prosecutor who refuses to speak to you? Or your coworker who always has a bad attitude? (Don't write their name here – you may want to loan them this book later).

It is so frustrating to deal with rude, belligerent, pessimistic, avoidant people when you're trying to respond to people who are suffering from trauma!

Are you catching on here?

All of these behaviors are trauma symptoms – the yelling, avoidance, bad attitude. So, what if that officer who you think is so mean is actually a survivor himself? And what if that prosecutor recently lost a family member to a serious illness or is being triggered by her cases?

We can be so much more effective (and sane) in our work if we learn to see all negative behavior through a "trauma lens." This means asking yourself, "I wonder what this person has gone through that caused this behavior?" And it also means practicing empathy and compassion when someone is struggling, rather than judgment and frustration.

One of my favorite quotes: "Be kind, for everyone is fighting a hard battle you know nothing about."[3]

At least half of people have some form of trauma in their past – and as you might imagine, the number is even higher for helping professionals. Then, factor in the trauma we often take in as part of our work, and we are walking around like the cast of the Walking Traumatized – totally triggered and totally unaware.

Does that excuse poor behavior or mistreatment of survivors? Of course not. But, it can certainly help you understand it. It can help you respond in a more compassionate way. And it might just help you build a new connection, and create a true ally.

So, when talking with that officer, rather than shutting down or getting defensive, you can say, "I hear your frustration. I really do. I can't imagine how difficult your job must be. I would love to hear about some of your experiences over lunch."

You've opened the door. You've started building a bridge. You've made him feel seen and heard – which is what everyone truly wants. And it's what we do for survivors each and every day. Why not extend that same compassion to everyone we meet and collaborate with?

Is there someone in your life you are struggling to connect with? Is there someone whose behavior frustrates and irritates you? (If not, send me an email, I'll loan you some of mine). If so, set a timer for two minutes, and write about what behavior bothers you, what might be causing it (though we can never fully know someone else's "why"), and how you might respond to it differently – and with more compassion.

_____

_____

_____

_____

_____

_____

_____

Chapter Four

Balancing the Scales

You already know that sexual and domestic violence are not about violence – they're about power. For these crimes to flourish, one person must be in a position of power over another, and make a conscious <u>choice</u> to exploit and abuse that power.

And as long as we allow inequality of any kind, these abuses will continue. This is why one of the most important keys to ending these epidemics is promoting equality. By doing so, we are helping to balance the scales. And the fact is, you can't abuse or rape someone who is your equal.

Power dynamics are kind of like a teeter totter (which, as a formerly clumsy child, is not my favorite analogy – but I digress). On a teeter totter, you move at the will of the heavier or stronger (more powerful) person. In sexual assault or domestic violence, the perpetrator is the more powerful person. The perpetrator holds all the power. The perpetrator holds down their end of the scale, while maintaining complete control over the victim's side as well.

Another image to think of is a scale – shifting back and forth depending on the amount of weight placed on each side. The only way for the survivor to ever have safety and autonomy is to reclaim power over her side of the scale. Our goal is to even out that scale: to hold the perpetrator accountable, reducing their power – while empowering the survivor, giving her power back to her.

So, how do we do that?

We start by truly *believing* that everyone is equal. And to do that, we need to unpack our own biases. Now, I know you are an intelligent, enlightened, progressive person – I mean, you chose this great book, after all. So, you hold absolutely no biases, right?

Wrong. We all have something we judge, look down upon, or just don't quite understand.

In my early years as an advocate, I discovered that I held some biases against very wealthy people. I come from, well … humble beginnings. I grew up poor – very poor. Roaches-in-my-cereal poor. And if I dared to complain, my grandmother (who raised me) would scoff and say, "Just brush them off, they didn't eat much." So yeah, *that poor.*

So, when women came into my tiny advocacy office in the courthouse basement decked out in designer clothes and diamonds, I would often think (never actually *say*, but often *think*) – *"psssht, yeah, like you really need my help."* Guess what that is? Yep, judgment.

I soon realized that these women were dealing with barriers I couldn't possibly imagine. Asking a woman to leave her apartment and move her children and one bag of belongings into a shelter is hard enough. Asking a woman to move from a 5,000 square foot home in the suburbs to the shelter may be even more difficult. Losing it all can be even more difficult when you have a lot to lose.

I also soon realized that living in a wealthy neighborhood and having a lot of *stuff* didn't mean she had any more access to her funds than the survivors who were living in poverty. Their partners still had all control over the finances – no matter how ample those finances may have been.

And wealthier women would also often talk about the fear of having police in their neighborhood. This is something I never had to worry about since, you know, police were *always* in my neighborhood. I soon realized that every victim's struggle is unique.

But even after this revelation, and countless others since, I still catch myself judging people on occasion. But now, I realize that anytime I'm judging someone, that's *my stuff*, not theirs. I realize now that judgment means I have another issue to unpack. And if I want to create a world where those scales (teeter totters) are balanced – and I absolutely do – it's my obligation to do the work to unpack these views, even when it's hard or painful. Because my judgment makes it harder for that survivor to be heard, believed, and empowered. Any judgment I carry about a survivor, or about anyone, becomes another weight on the perpetrator's side of the scale. And if we do nothing else in this work, we should at least make sure we are <u>not</u> working for the perpetrators.

Now, the fact is, you won't necessarily *like* all survivors, and that's okay. You don't have to like someone to believe they deserve to be respected, safe, and free to make their own decisions. But, you do have to truly believe that they deserve these things – and truly see them as our equal.

I once worked with a survivor who was covered in racist tattoos – KKK symbols, swastikas all over her forearms. It was shocking. And some of the language that she used was even more shocking. She had been raped and beaten by her husband for years, and was ready to get away. She needed support – and we (my fellow advocates and I) were there to provide it.

I sat with her during the criminal trial, helped her get an order of protection, and supported her as she started working toward a divorce. She would share with me that she was starting to question some of her racist views. Her husband was the member of a racist hate group and had tried to convince her that his beliefs were true. But, the further away she got from him, the more it all seemed ridiculous to her.

She came back to visit me a few months later, on her way to her final divorce hearing. For the first time, she noticed a picture of my daughter on my desk – my gorgeous, then infant, *half-African* daughter. The woman's face immediately turned red. She felt ashamed. She said, "Oh my gosh, how on earth did you work with me?" I smiled, paused, and joked, "sometimes it was hard, hun." She smiled. "But, truly, I believe you are a great person, and you absolutely deserve to be safe and respected. I'm so proud of you for all you have accomplished." She smiled again, and thanked me.

Everyone reading this probably knows how rare it is to have these moments – when a survivor comes back to thank you or to tell you about the impact you have had on his or her life. But, when it happens, it's the most magical feeling in the world.

It didn't matter that I disagreed with her or that I had serious concerns about her views. What mattered is that this woman who had been beaten down (literally) for so long was now free. She felt empowered, and she was safe. And the really magical part? By feeling more empowered herself, she started to see others as her equals, too. Now, I'm not saying she's marching in NAACP parades or working to fight racism, but she did start to question her oppressive beliefs, all because someone (advocates!) believed and validated her. See how powerful advocacy can be?

I said that all struggles are unique, but I won't say that all struggles are equal. There are some survivors who are facing real life-generated challenges and oppression that make it even more difficult to ever balance out the scale. Women of color, LGBTQ+ survivors, survivors with disabilities, foreign-born survivors, incarcerated survivors, Native American survivors all have very real oppression they have to encounter each and every day. Each of these forms of oppression are an extra weight on the side of the perpetrator. So, in these instances, it is our job as advocates to work even harder to balance the scales – through effective outreach, culturally appropriate services, and working to fight oppression on a daily basis.

One way to think about our work as it relates to eradicating oppression is to picture all forms of violence as branches on a tree – domestic violence, sexual assault, human trafficking, child abuse, hate crimes, etc… These branches are, unfortunately, flourishing. And we spend most of our daily work trying to prune back these branches, by holding perpetrators accountable and supporting survivors.

But, what happens when you prune the branches of a tree? They grow back, right? And they often grow back even

stronger than before. If you truly want to get rid of a tree –
this tree of violence[4] – altogether, you have to focus on the
roots.

And for this tree, the roots are all forms of oppression:
racism, sexism, homophobia, transphobia, ageism, ableism,
xenophobia. Basically, the roots that keep this tree
flourishing are any system or belief that keeps one person
in a position of power over another.

We not only have to uproot the biases and oppression
that's present in the systems in which we work, but we also
have to consciously unpack all of the biases we hold,
because we too are contributing to these poisonous roots.

Here are a few common types of judgmental and
oppressive thoughts and beliefs I'd like you to watch out

for:

1. "I don't condone or support their lifestyle (choice, etc.), but I treat everyone the same." This is often said about the LGBTQ+ community. And I implore you, if you have deeply-held beliefs about this, please assess where these beliefs came from, and work them out. If you cannot or will not rethink your views, please choose another line of work.

That may sound harsh, but believing that someone is wrong for *who they are* is oppressive – and creates inequality. These views create tremendous advantages for perpetrators. You're practically standing on the perpetrator's side of the scale. And remember, if you do nothing else as an advocate, at least make sure you're not working for the perpetrator. So, please, find a way to work this out.

2. **"They just don't' know any better."** I have heard this said about both victims/survivors and perpetrators. Either way, it's offensive. It's oppressive. And it must stop.

Survivors are not to blame for the violence they endure, so it has nothing to do with how much or how little they know. And perpetrators absolutely already know enough to have power and control over someone. They do have a lot yet to learn – or, to unlearn – but that is certainly not a justification for their actions.

I have also heard this statement in relation to survivors or perpetrators from other cultures or nationalities. People often mistakenly believe that people from other nations are more violent, or tolerate more violence, simply because their culture allows it. But, do you know whose culture actually allows and supports this type of violence? *Ours.*

As someone who has worked with many immigrant and foreign-born survivors, I can assure you that most experienced much more violence *after* coming to the United States. They are not tolerating the violence, they are simply facing incredible barriers to getting away. These barriers include isolation, lack of appropriate language access, and blatant discrimination from service providers. It is not a matter of "not knowing any better," it is a matter of not having enough choices or resources.

And while it is true that some nations do not have adequate laws in place to address sexual and domestic violence (though, arguably, neither does the U.S.), that does not mean that perpetrators from these cultures are not still making a <u>choice</u> to abuse or rape. It is essential that we never justify somcone's harmful and violent behavior because of our own lack of understanding about their culture.

3. **"Victims just have low self-esteem."** By the time she comes into your office, that statement may be true. Anyone would have low self-esteem (whatever that means) after being beaten, raped, ridiculed, manipulated, and degraded. That's kind of the point of what the perpetrator is doing. But, I can assure you she did not start out that way.

One of the most powerful questions you can ask a victim is: "Tell me what your life looked like before you met him/her?" It is a great way for the survivor to remember and recognize the impact of the violence, and also for us to see a glimpse of the truly strong, resilient person sitting in front of us.

Have you spotted any judgments you hold? If so, set a timer for two minutes, and write about them here. Where did it come from? Are you judging people against your own experiences (like me with my cereal roaches)?

This is not about judging or being hard on yourself. It's about becoming aware, so you can start to unpack that box, too.

_____

_____

_____

_____

Now, how do these judgments connect to how you're

judging yourself? Because, I assure you – they do. For

example, if you are a parent and you find yourself judging

other parents for how they dress, feed, or treat their

children – it is probably because of your own guilt or

insecurity about your own parenting.

I promise you, our judgments are almost always really

about ourselves. Remember, any time we judge someone,

it is *our stuff.* So, take a couple of minutes and be

reeeeaaally honest with yourself. What are you *really*

judging? And can we let that go, too?

_____

_____

_____

_____

_____

_____

_____

_____

_____

_____

Whew! Unpacking boxes is hard work. But, don't you feel

a bit relieved – and more empowered – already?

Chapter Five

Giving Them What They *Really* Need

As advocates, we spend countless hours listening, guiding, and empowering. We sit beside survivors during court proceedings. We welcome parents and children into shelter and help them feel (as much as possible) at home. We attend meetings to forge relationships with collaborative partners. We scrounge up resources where there seems to be none available. And we are constantly looking for new and innovative ways to truly help the survivors we serve.

Remember in Chapter One, we talked about that incredible urge you felt to do something – *anything!* – to help survivors? It is that insatiable urge that keeps us in the work and keeps us lying awake at night, trying to figure out new ways to make a difference.

In trainings, advocates are constantly asking for new resources, new tools, and new approaches to make survivors' lives, and their jobs, easier and more manageable. I get it. I've spent much of my career searching for solutions too. But, I eventually realized that we've been searching for solutions in all the wrong places – when the true answer was available to us all along.

Let me explain by sharing a story about how I discovered this answer. (Trigger warning: the following story is about child sexual abuse, disclosure, and a suicide attempt). When I was two years old, my mother sent me to live with her mother and step-father. She wasn't able to raise me because, at that time, she was too dependent on drugs, alcohol, and an abusive man (my father). She sent me to live with people who she thought would love and care for me: her parents. Unfortunately, she was wrong.

My step-grandfather started sexually abusing me when I was five. At least, that's my earliest memory of him coming in my room at night and making me "play" with him. I remember tucking myself in as tightly as I could, hoping that my blanket armor might be too difficult for him to maneuver. It never worked. And instead, I would often be left there after his visits, or on nights he chose not to visit, having a vivid nightmare about being smothered by a blanket.

I had that nightmare until my late 20s.

When I was eleven, we moved from our small house in the city to a converted trailer in the country. We were further away from civilization, and he was further away from being caught. At around that time, I started fighting back, demanding that he stop touching me or I was going to tell. But, I never did.

He tried various tactics to keep me quiet. He threatened me. He threatened my grandmother, my dog, anyone I cared about. He made me watch as he killed a litter of puppies, and then made me bury them. He tried everything to scare me, to silence me. But, he didn't realize that his tactics had nothing to do with why I didn't tell.

I never told because I knew no one would believe me. I never told because I didn't think I deserved to be safe. What was happening to me was supposed to happen, because I was bad and I deserved it. I didn't tell because I thought I didn't matter.

There was no story to tell.

When I was 15, I decided I didn't want to live anymore. I went into the bathroom, took out every pill bottle I could find, and dumped their contents on the counter. And then, the phone rang. I answered it so the ringing wouldn't disturb my grandmother.

"Pam? Are you ok?"

The caller was a friend from school. A friend I talked with often, but had never told about what was happening in my home. She said "something just said I should call."

I dropped the phone, walked into the kitchen, and told my grandmother I needed to talk to her. I decided to tell her that day because *something* told my friend to call. And my friend cared enough to pick up the phone.

Something, someone believed I shouldn't kill myself.
Someone felt like I deserved to live, like maybe I even had
a purpose. Something, someone believed *I mattered*.

So now, there was something to tell.

Before I could even speak the words, my grandmother
laughed, turned her back and snarled, "Let me guess, he
molested you?" She knew. She had always known. She
threw me out of the house that day, and I never went back.
I was scared and alone. But, I made it through high school,
college, law school, and started a career and family—
because *I knew that I mattered*. It hasn't been easy. But, even
when memories came back to haunt me, or my past caused
challenges (because of those pesky trauma boxes), I felt in

my heart that I truly mattered. And that has been enough to get me through.

I've discovered over the past several years in this work that people are searching for this same message: We all want to know we matter.

Perpetrators are skilled at making victims feel that they don't matter – often because of their own perceived lack of worth. The abusive spouse will make their partner feel invisible, stupid, crazy, irrational, afraid – unworthy. The rapist makes his victim feel invaded, degraded, unheard, unseen – unworthy.

And unfortunately, in the past 40 years of this work we have done little to turn this around In fact, we have been able to save the lives of more abusers than victims – largely because women have more safe places to go, so not as many victims have to resort to killing the abuser in self-defense.

We have made incredible progress in offering safe housing, employment, legal protections, and other resources – though we still have a long way to go. But, these resources are never going to be enough if we aren't also helping survivors – and those who have not yet been victimized – feel worthy.

The woman who is being abused by her husband will not reach out, regardless of how many services we have to offer, if she feels that she does not matter. Just like myself as a child, she will feel there's no story to tell.

She may reach out for her children's well-being, but it will be very difficult for her to engage in systems and to fully participate in our services if she herself feels she does not matter. And if we make the mistake, as we often do, of trying to make decision for her, we are, albeit unintentionally, contributing to her feelings of worthlessness.

So, what can we do?

We can start by believing that we are equal to every survivor, and every person (see Chapter Four). We can focus on recognizing each person's strength and resiliency – and helping them see it, as well. We can respect and honor every person's decisions – even when we don't agree with them. After all, it's his/her life, and it's not about us.

We have to truly believe that every survivor, and every

person, matters – including ourselves.

So, what does it mean to matter? Knowing that you matter means knowing you deserve love and respect. It means knowing that people will believe you and stand up for your rights. It means knowing that you are as valuable and important as every other person on this planet.

Can you imagine how powerful that message would be, if everyone received it? And we, as advocates, have tremendous power to change people's lives, simply by helping them see their own worth. How cool is that?

Did you ever receive the message that you did not matter? If so, how has that impacted you today? And how might it be impacting your work with survivors? Set a timer for two minutes and write about that here.

Chapter Six

Stopping It Before It Starts

As advocates, we are often focused on the intervention side of the work – responding to violence after it happens. But, as we know, we will never change these epidemics unless we also focus on preventing them.

To get us started thinking about prevention, let's begin with the famous river parable. Once upon a time there was a small village on the edge of a river. Life in the village was good. But one day, a villager noticed a baby floating down the river. The villager quickly swam out to save the baby from drowning.

The next day, this same villager noticed two babies in the river. He called for help, and both babies were rescued.

And the following day, four babies were seen caught in the

turbulent current. And then eight, then more, and still

more!

The villagers organized themselves quickly, setting up

watchtowers and training teams of swimmers who could

resist the swift waters and rescue babies.

Rescue squads were soon working 24 hours a day. And

each day, the number of helpless babies floating down the

river increased. The villagers organized themselves

efficiently. The rescue squads were now saving many

children each day. While not all the babies, now very

numerous, could be saved, the villagers felt they were doing

well to save as many as they could.

One day, however, someone raised the question, "But

where are all these babies coming from? Let's organize a team to head upstream to find out who's throwing all of these babies into the river in the first place!"[5]

Aha! Let's work on stopping this epidemic before it starts. Wouldn't that be nice?

I've never felt that babies floating down a river was the most empowering image, but it does illustrate an important point. If we keep focusing only on all the work we have to do, we will always have more work. If we keep plucking babies out of the river (offering survivors resources), we will always have more and more babies (survivors).

I know that my goal is to work myself out of a job. I would love to be able to focus on puppies or travel or some other fun endeavor, because these epidemics just no longer exist.

Can you imagine how incredible life would be if everyone was truly safe?

One of my favorite images comes from the "Truth is Beauty" sculpture created by Marco Cochrane,[6] which was displayed at the 2013 Burning Man festival.

This is Cochrane's description of his inspiration for "Truth is Beauty":

"As a child I was deeply affected by the abduction and violation of one of my friends. I thought, the man that did that to her must not have realized she was a real person. I have been trying to solve this problem my entire life through my art. The women I sculpt are safe, present. Look at them. They have chosen their own expression, so you will see

the actual woman, the person, her energy and spirit. You will see past

that part of her that has been objectified and used to disempower.

With the female body exposed and demystified it is the emotion, the

individual, the energy, the strength, the power, the beauty, the person

that remains. It is my intent that these sculptures exude this healing

energy and inspire us to take action; to finally say enough is enough."

"Truth is Beauty" is the second in a series of three

monumental sculptures by Marco Cochrane. These

sculptures are intended to demand a change in perspective,

to be catalysts for social change, to de-objectify women and

inspire men and women to take action to end violence

against women, thus allowing both women and men to live

fully and safely.

The sculpture pushes us to imagine a world where all

women and girls (and inevitably, all people) are safe and

free, completely free of any worry of victimization or

exploitation. It may sound like the stuff of unicorns and mermaids, but I truly believe it can – and will – happen. And that belief is what keeps me going in this work, each and every day. (It's my *why*).

Imagine how different your life and the lives of those around you would be if sexual assault and domestic violence did not exist. Really, I want you to imagine it. What would it be like to walk down the street without having to assess your level of safety? What would it be like to never have to wonder if your date may try to control or abuse you? What would it be like to never have to worry when your children go outside to play? Really, imagine it. Then, write about this image here.

Aaaaaahhhh. Sounds pretty incredible, right? So, how do we get there?

First, we have to recognize the true causes of these epidemics: Inequality and abuse of power. To get to the core of this issue, we need to understand two concepts – privilege and oppression. These are hard topics to talk about, because they tend to cause people to feel defensive, guilty, or shut down. But, I'm asking you to keep an open mind and heart, and truly think about how these forces interact in each or our lives.

Privilege consists of any unearned benefits. For example, I identify as white – as evidenced by my glowing pale skin and frequent sun burns. Because we live in a culture that is still racist, I receive some unearned and unfair benefits because of the color of my skin.

For example, I can drive through nearly any town in American and not be afraid. I can shop nearly anywhere and not be followed around the store. In fact, once when I was a poor and not-too-bright teenager, I walked into a store with an empty bottle of shampoo and exchanged it for a full one (ie, I stole it)– with not even a raised eyebrow from the staff.

I share this story for two reasons. One, because I believe the statute of limitations on that crime has expired – phew![7] And two, because I truly believe the outcome would have been much different if I was African American or Latina.

This is not, of course, to say that all white people have it easy. I have already shared with you that I have been abused, homeless, and poor. But, I know that I also had a lot of advantages. In most job interviews, I have shared the same skin color as the boss who was interviewing me.

Even if subconsciously, this provided me with a benefit.

And perhaps the biggest privilege of all: I am able to walk

through life without worrying about racism, if I choose not

to.

We know that no one is completely privileged or

completely oppressed – we have all experienced some form

of discrimination, due to our ethnicity, gender, income,

ability status, sexual orientation, or some other trait that

society has deemed "less than." And we all have some

level of privilege based on what society has deemed "better

than."

For example, a white women (such as myself) experiences

both sexism (oppression) and white privilege. So, while I

may not feel in danger because of my skin color, I

absolutely am aware of the danger posed by my gender. Of course, we are all multi-faceted, multi-dimensional people. So we all have multiple layers of privilege and oppression that we experience on a daily basis.

The best illustration I have heard of privilege and oppression comes from a dear friend, former colleague, and brilliant advocate and professor, Stacey Mann. Stacey describes privilege and oppression as being like riding a bike. Inequality is like the wind. If you are privileged, the wind is at your back – it is helping you. You are riding your bike effortlessly, pedaling along without even breaking a sweat. When the wind is at your back, you don't even have to acknowledge that it's windy. You can just think that you are *really good* at riding that bike, without ever noticing that you're getting a lot of help.

But, when you're oppressed, the wind is at your face —

holding you back. You have to pedal faster, work harder,

and try much more to get anywhere. You are very much

aware of the wind — because you are battling it every day.

If you are realizing, perhaps for the first time, that you have

some wind at your back (privilege), don't fret! This is not a

reason to feel guilty. Because again, you did not earn it or

cause it. You did not ask for it. And now that you realize

you have it, which is more than most people will ever do,

you can decide how to use it.

You can just enjoy it — because hey, it feels good to have

the wind at your back! You can abuse it, which is what

perpetrators choose to do — taking advantage of the

privilege they hold (as men, as able-bodied people, etc.).

Or, you can use that knowledge and power to become an

ally, and fight against oppression. This is what I, and many of my dear colleagues, have chosen to do. And it is what I hope you will choose to do as well.

We also have to realize how this privilege and oppression are created. Let's focus, for now, on male privilege and the collective sexism or oppression of women and girls. How does this happen?

We live in a society that teaches boys they are worthy only if they are powerful, while teaching girls they are worthy only if they are likeable. We encourage boys to embrace their power and girls to give their power away, in exchange for popularity and acceptance.

This system results in the scales being off balance as early as elementary school – where boys are being taught to be strong and girls are being taught to be nice. And by middle school, boys are being taught to have power *over* others, while girls are being taught to sit quietly, not speak up, and hope someone likes them.

And while this system does create a lot of privilege (wind at their backs) for men and boys, it is also harming them. This insistence on power results in boys not feeling safe expressing emotion. It leaves boys not being able to lean on one another for support and comfort. And it causes boys in the U.S. to be more likely to be diagnosed with a behavior disorder, prescribed stimulant medications, fail out of school, binge drink, commit a violent crime, and/or take their own lives.[8]

Boys who are taught they do not have the right to cry when they are hurt grow up not knowing how to feel pain. They grow up not knowing how to handle pain when their high school girlfriend breaks up with them, or when their boss fires them.

Boys and men who have not been taught how to properly feel and process emotions will react with the only emotion they've been given permission to feel: Anger. So, when that teenage boy feels sad and hurt, rather than cry and mourn the loss of the relationship, he will likely lash out—often at his former girlfriend.

Also, boys are constantly criticized for doing something (anything) "like a girl." For example, "stop throwing like a girl," or "stop playing with that doll." When we criticize a boy for doing something like a girl, we are teaching him that to be like a girl is bad, and that girls are *less than* boys. These messages create a culture of shame in our children. Girls are raised knowing they are seen as less valuable than boys, and boys are raised ashamed that they can never be quite manly enough.

We have to stop raising boys who feel worthless because they can never seem to reach this unattainable vision of "manhood." We are raising young men who are filled with shame, and who believe they are better than women. So, it should be no surprise that these men often grow up and learn to let all of that aggression out—usually on women.

Think about the message you received about what it means to be a man or a woman? How have these messages impacted your life?

If you are transgender or non-binary (not identifying as male or female), these messages can be even more confusing and damaging.

These flawed and oppression-ridden messages not only create inequalities, they also create fertile ground for domestic violence and sexual assault to flourish. To balance the scales, and prevent these epidemics, we have to change and reprogram these messages – in our children, and within ourselves.

Chapter Seven

Standing Your Ground

Before anyone starts writing a complaint letter, let me be clear: I am not talking about "stand your ground" gun laws. (Perhaps that's a topic for another book). I'm talking about standing our ground as advocates, as professionals – *as experts.*

Think about all the systems you have to navigate in your quest to support survivors: law enforcement, prosecutors, judges, nurses, hospital administrators, landlords, military personnel, etc.. And let's face it, we're not always treated with the most respect.

I remember walking into a training I was facilitating and overhearing an investigator whispering to her colleague, "oh great, an advocacy training. She's probably going to tell us to hug more."

I ignored it, but I had two thoughts about that comment:

1. *Actually, I'm here to teach you about epidemics that I happen to be an expert in, and provide you with tools to make you better at your job – thank you very much; and*

2. *What the hell is wrong with hugs?!*

The point is, advocates are sometimes seen as touchy-feely extras – someone to connect the victim with when you don't know what else to do with them, or when you don't feel like dealing with the tough (ie, human) stuff.
But, *we* all know – or we should know – that we are so much more. An advocate is often the first person a survivor confides in, the first person to be let into the

highly-selective and very fragile trust bubble. And without us carefully paving a way into that bubble, every other player in the system would be left helplessly locked out.

We are also the conduit – connecting often broken and disheveled systems and processes. We help people understand one another, and understand survivors.

Wow, we are awesome, right?

It's important that we remember that. It is essential that we treat ourselves, and expect others to treat us, as experts. Just as all people are equal to one another, we are equal to all professionals we work with. So, we must see ourselves as such.

Now, as we talked about in Chapter Three, it is also

important to treat our collaborative partners with respect and compassion. We must see their difficult behavior through a Trauma Lens, and work to get to know, and understand, them better.

But, playing nice and showing compassion does *not* mean allowing your boundaries to be compromised, or allowing yourself to be disrespected. Stand up for yourself – and for all advocates. Your work matters.

YOU matter.

Chapter Eight

Using Your Secret Weapon

As victim advocates, we are all skilled at helping others. We are experts at finding resources, even when there are none. We may not be able to turn water into wine (though that would be soo helpful), but we can absolutely turn one tiny shelter room into a comfortable home for a family of six. And that is pretty impressive. Whoever coined the expression "you can't get blood from a turnip" obviously never met an advocate – because we can squeeze resources out of anything.

And we are so very smart, too! We know protection order laws backward and forward and can get people the rights they deserve. We know the Power and Control Wheel (all

728 of them) by heart. We know all about victims' rights. And we understand the often crippling effects of trauma.

We have also, out of necessity, become skilled at efficiently completing detailed time logs, writing compelling grant narratives, and pitching our programs to foundations and legislators. We truly are experts. But, somewhere in the journey to become recognized professionals – with grant requirements, 501(c)(3) statuses, and medal name tags! – we have forgotten where we came from.

Advocacy did not start as a structured organization with framed diplomas on the wall. It started as women, seeing and feeling the deep pain being lived by their sisters, taking one another into their homes and hearts. Here is a rough timeline of some of our advocacy roots:

1950- Civil rights and anti-war movements challenge the

60s   country and lay the foundation for the feminist

        movement.

1970   The first battered women's shelter opens in

        Chiswick, England, by Erin Pizzey.

1971   The first rape crisis center opens in the United

        States by the Bay Area Women Against Rape.

1973   The first battered women's shelter in the United

        States opens in St. Paul, Minnesota, by the Women's

        Advocates.

Though I imagine women have been reaching out to their

sisters in need since the beginning of time. I imagine that

when a cave woman heard that another cave woman's male

partner hit her, she invited her friend into her cave, cooked

her up some nice grub (or grub worms) over the fire, and

then threw rocks at the husband when he wasn't looking.

(History was not my best subject).

The point is: Women have always had each other's backs —
thankfully.

And I can assure you that during those early years of
advocacy, one woman did not come to another and say,
"Sure, you can stay at my house, but we'll need you to
complete a few intake forms and go over the curfew policy.
Then we'll discuss your medical and legal options."
Instead, she probably said, "I'm sorry you're hurting. I'm
here for you." (And maybe she still threw rocks at the
husband).

She didn't worry about her friend's legal options or liability.
She listened and sincerely cared. She walked beside her
sister as she healed — in whatever way made sense for her.

I'm not suggesting that we throw out our intake forms –

though I so wish we could! And I am certainly not telling

you not to worry about liability (please don't have your

Board of Directors call me). But, I am suggesting – no,

imploring – us all to return to our advocacy roots.

I believe that the most powerful tools we have are not

about resources or options or any of our professional

expertise. They come simply from our own human

connection – from being able to truly feel and share in the

pain of another.

Empathy: That is truly our secret weapon – always has

been, always will be.

So, even without funders and grant requirements, and all

the systems we must navigate, we can still turn to our sister or brother who is hurting, whose life has been turned

upside down, and say, "I am here." And these words, this

feeling, will be just as powerful today as it was in 1950 (or

700BC).

Brené Brown describes empathy as "feeling with someone."

She also brilliantly distinguishes it from sympathy, which is

feeling sorry *for* someone.[9] Isn't that a powerful

distinction? And Sheryl Sandburg, in the aftermath of

losing her beloved husband, reflected on what she has

learned about empathy. She stated that, "Real empathy is

sometimes not insisting that it will be okay but

acknowledging that it is not."[10]

Empathy is about validation and connection, not solutions.

Empathetic things to say to a survivor may include:

- Thank you for telling me.

- I believe you.

- This is not your fault.

- I'm here.

- You are not alone.

- And even, "that really stinks."

Empathy isn't always pretty or eloquent, but it is always powerful. And it is truly the most effective tool we have to help survivors heal. It is our superpower.

Chapter Nine

Filling Your Cup

"My coffee cup is empty. Maybe yours is, too. But through grace and the beauty of the universe, I know that I will likely drink again soon. Life is like that. But here's the secret: YOU have to get up and get your own coffee. Sometimes, someone who loves you very much will fill the cup. But more times than not, that's YOUR job. Fill your cup."

~ Chris Brogan

As we discussed in previous chapters, the only way we can help someone heal is to empathize – to feel *with them*. But, this is risky business. To truly empathize, we have to connect with the part of us that remembers what pain truly feels like. We have to not only connect with and feel the survivor's pain, we have to connect with and feel *our own*. And since many of us in helping professions have a history of trauma, this connection can often lead to triggers, re-experiencing, and a renewal of our own trauma symptoms. This is why it is essential that we find ways to process our own trauma, through self-care.

Self-care is one of those catch phrases that is thrown around a lot. But, we don't often take time to really stop and think about what it means. Self-care literally means to *focus on caring for yourself.* So, rather than spending all of your time providing compassion and support for survivors, your friends, your family, and everyone else, it means truly stopping and taking time to provide compassion and support *for you.*

My dear friend and colleague, Olga Phoenix, has created an incredible model to help us all bring more self-care into our lives. The "Self-Care Wheel" illustrates the various facets of our lives, as well as suggestions for how to love and care for ourselves more in each of these areas.[11]

SELF-CARE
WHEEL

For me, self-care also means sometimes being a bit selfish. It means recognizing that there are things I could be doing for other people, but instead, I consciously choose to do something *for me.*

Sometimes this means simply relaxing: taking a bubble bath, napping, or (one of my personal favorites) curling up on the couch with a Golden Girls marathon (don't judge me).

We have been mistakenly taught that being "selfish" is wrong. When, in fact, if we don't sometimes focus on ourselves, we will never be able to give our full potential to anyone else.

But, sometimes, self-care is about filling yourself up (filling your own cup). This means doing things that make you feel truly inspired, energetic, and empowered.

So, what do you love to do?

If you cannot easily come up with an answer to that question, or if your answer involved other people (working, spending time with family, etc.), you have some work to do, my friend.

We all need things we can do *on our own* that fill up our cup. If you don't know what those things are, think about what you loved to do as a child. This will often point you toward the activities that are most empowering for you.

For me, though much of my childhood was painful, I always felt joyful and at peace when I was writing – especially if I was writing outside. And today, this is still one of my favorite things to do. If I start to feel stressed –

or even before I start to feel stressed, because prevention! –

I take my journal outside and spend a few minutes (or

longer) writing. I don't necessarily have to write about

anything in particular – I just write.

I have also always loved to dance. (I wanted to be a dancer

for the NBA when I was younger. Let's all be grateful that

didn't pan out). And today, I often take work breaks and

dance around my office. I also find time to go out dancing

with friends whenever possible. Dancing makes me feel

happy and empowered – so I make time for it. Because *I*

matter.

How do you take care of yourself? And what activities did

you used to love, that you can bring back into your life

today? Set a timer for two minutes and write about it here.

It is also important to realize that, sometimes, a bubble bath and dancing just won't be enough. Over the years, I have talked with countless advocates who are struggling in their careers. They feel completely dedicated to the work to end sexual assault and domestic violence. But, they feel exhausted by grant requirements, battles with collaborative partners, long hours, lack of self-care, endless red tape, and burned out supervisors.

Sometimes this exhaustion is due to unpacked trauma boxes, and taking on additional trauma each time we work with a survivor. Sometimes this exhaustion is due to burn out – which is truly about feeling disconnected to the mission of your work. Whatever the reason, exhaustion is real. It makes us dread going to work every morning. And no one deserves to live that way.

I understand the struggle of wanting so desperately to help survivors, but feeling like you just can't be in this work one more day. I reached that point a few years ago, as I was leading a statewide organization. I agonized over the decision to leave. I felt like a traitor, like I was giving up. But, in the end, I realized that I was being a hypocrite by telling survivors and my staff to take care of themselves, while I was working at 3am. I also realized that I no longer felt supported by my superiors. I wanted to do the work in a way that I knew I was making a difference – and I just couldn't do so in that position anymore.

If you have done the work to unpack your own trauma boxes, and you have committed to taking better care of yourself, but you still feel resentful, deflated, and exhausted in your job – it may be time for a change, my friend. I want you to remember something: Being an advocate has nothing to do with your job title. It is part of who you are.

So, no matter what you do for a living, where you work, or what title you hold, as long as you are committed to empowering survivors, holding perpetrators accountable, and working to end these epidemics – you, my friend, are an advocate. Always have been, always will be. No one can change that.

Of course, I want you to stay in the work. You are incredible! And we need you. But, more importantly, I want you to be happy. I want you to feel truly inspired and empowered each and every day – because you deserve that. You deserve to feel like what you are doing is making a difference. You deserve to feel appreciated. And if you don't feel that way in your current position, you have every right to leave.

Remember, as we discussed in Chapter Five, advocacy is about empowering people to know and believe that they matter. But, part of that means knowing and believing that *we matter too.* So, if you have learned nothing else from this book (though I hope you have), please at least remember this:

All people deserve to be treated with respect. All people deserve empathy and compassion. And all people deserve to be safe and happy – *including you.*

Because I want you to really understand how incredible you are, I have a special request. Please use this last two-minute writing exercise to write a "thank you" letter to a very important person – YOU. Thank yourself for all you do every day. Thank yourself for all the things you do that you think go unnoticed. And thank yourself for just being you.

You deserve it.

_____

_____

_____

_____

_____

_____

_____

_____

_____

_____

_____

_____

_____

_____

_____

_____

_____

_____

It feels good to be appreciated, doesn't it? And the great

thing is, we never have to wait for anyone else to say

"thank you," we can always say (or write) it to ourselves.

So, before we end (because I just don't want to go!), here is

one final "thank you" – from me to you.

Dear advocate,

Thank you for being here. Thank you for spending your hard-earned resources on this book. And thank you for taking the time to read these pages. I truly appreciate it.

Most of all, thank you for all you do to help people feel seen, heard, and worthy. Thank you for meeting people during their darkest moments and helping them see that they still shine. Thank you for helping to turn fear into hope, and heartbreak into healing. You are truly magical.

Thank you for all that you do, each and every day. You *are* making a difference. You are changing and saving lives. Truly, you are changing the world, one survivor at a time. And as a woman, mother, and a survivor – I thank you.

Finally, thank you for taking good care of yourself. Thank you for protecting a very important person, who we need so very much. Please remember how very precious and important you are.

You matter, my friend. Please never forget it.

Love,

Pam

NOTES

About the Author

Pamela Jacobs is an *advocate*. She has dedicated her career to empowering survivors and working to end sexual and domestic violence. She is also an attorney, speaker, and writer – using each of these platforms to further this work and inspire social change.

Pamela has worked with survivors for over 15 years, and currently speaks to audiences nationwide about how to respond to and prevent these epidemics. Prior to launching Pamela Jacobs Consulting in 2013, Pamela served as the Executive Director of a statewide sexual assault and domestic violence coalition, and as an attorney serving immigrant and traditionally underserved survivors.

Pamela began her advocacy career as a court advocate with a YWCA – where she learned that advocacy is much less about *fixing* than it is about simply *listening*. She also witnessed first-hand the re-victimization that often occurs in the court process. This is what inspired her to become an attorney – though she still considers herself to be an advocate "with more student loans."

In her sought-after speaking events, Pamela utilizes empathy, connection, humor, and her own experiences as a survivor to inspire and empower audiences to create change in their homes, organizations, schools, and communities. She is also a regular contributor to the Huffington Post and an Expert Writer on Toxic Relationship Support for About.com.

Pamela received her Juris Doctorate from Washburn University School of Law, and currently resides in North Carolina with her daughter and rescued pets. For more information, please visit http://pamelajacobs.com.

Acknowledgements

This was one of the most difficult sections to write, because there are so many people I want to thank! If I truly listed everyone I am grateful for, I would fill another book. So, I'll do my best to keep this brief ...

First, I am forever grateful for my daughter, Juke, who is my inspiration for this book, my work, and everything I do. I carry this torch so that, one day, she and her peers will never have to be afraid. And I am incredibly proud to see her picking up the torch and fighting for justice and social change, as well.

To my dear friend, Bobbie Jo Adkins (builtbybobbie.com) who not only designed the book cover, webpage, and marketing materials for The Empowered Advocate™, but who has also been a constant source of support and encouragement as I procrastinated writing and finishing this book: You are a lifesaver, my friend.

To my many beloved friends and colleagues who have been by my side throughout this process, and throughout my advocacy journey, I hope you know I much I truly appreciate you. There are far too many of you to name everyone individually, but I suspect you know who you are!

I also want to thank everyone who reviewed this book before it went to press: Melissa Seligman, Kathy Ray, Olga Phoenix, Hope Dyer, Laura Patzner, Tracy Bowie, Aquisha Gross, and Misty Campbell – your time, thoughtful consideration, and feedback are greatly appreciated. You made this a better book, and me a better writer.

I am incredibly thankful for each advocate in The Empowered Advocate Facebook group, where we support, encourage, and inspire one another. Thank you all!

And, of course, I want to thank everyone who is reading this. Thank you for the work you do, and thank you for who you are. I wrote this book for *you*, because you are truly my (s)hero. Keep fighting, friend. There is much work yet to be done.

This may be the end of the book, but it is absolutely not goodbye! I hope you will all stay connected with me. You can find me online at http://pamelajacobs.com or on Facebook at www.facebook.com/pamelajacobsconsulting. You can also email me at pam@pamelajacobs.com. And hopefully I'll see you at a speaking event soon!

Remember, friend:

YOU matter!

[1] If you have not already done so, I encourage you to watch Dr. Rebecca Campbell's lecture on the Neurobiology of Trauma. It is conveniently available online at https://www.youtube.com/watch?v=mTOZE90-fCY.

[2] Of course, this belief that a sexual assault survivor is lying is also perpetrated by victim blaming and rape culture, but that's a topic for another discussion. I recommend this one:
Yes Means Yes!: Visions of Female Sexual Power & A World Without Rape, collection of essays edited by Jessica Valenti and Jaclyn Friedman.

[3] This quote is often attributed to Plato, though the true origin is unknown.

[4] In 2012, the South Dakota Coalition Ending Domestic & Sexual Violence created three new tools: the Battering Triangle, Equality Wheel, and Violence/ Non-violence Tree, based upon the work of Sacred Circle & DAIP of Duluth. The Violence/Non-Violence Tree graphic is available online at http://www.ncall.us/sites/ncall.us/files/resources/Violence-Non-Violence%20Tree.pdf.

[5] The "River Story" is a common way to describe primary prevention. This story is also often called "The Upstream Story." It highlights the need to address the roots causes of a health problem. Some attribute it to the community organizer Saul Alinsky. Some people refer to it as a traditional story or as the "public health parable." Learn more at http://wiki.preventconnect.org/River+Story.

[6] Learn more about this sculpture, and more of Marco Cochrane's work, at http://www.marcocochranesculpture.net/.

[7] Note: To any teenagers reading this, I want to emphasize what a bad decision this was. While I was able to walk out of the store without being caught, my purse was stolen the next day – causing me to forever believe in the existence of karma, and never to steal again.

[8] For a great analysis of the crisis facing boys in America, check out the groundbreaking documentary, "The Mask You Live In" by The Representation Project. Learn more at http://therepresentationproject.org/film/the-mask-you-live-in.

[9] Brene Brown, TEDx Houston: The Power of Vulnerability, filmed June 2010, *available at* https://www.ted.com/talks/brene_brown_on_vulnerability?language=en.

[10] Sheryl Sandberg's heartfelt letter about the passing of her husband is available here http://time.com/3907655/sheryl-sandberg-letter-husband/.

[11] Olga Phoenix is a phenomenal speaker, author, advocate, and survivor who has dedicated her career to helping advocates and other helpers lead lives free of vicarious trauma. You can find her on Facebook at https://www.facebook.com/OlgaPhoenixProject. I also highly recommend her book, Victim Advocate's Guide to Wellness:: Six Dimensions of Vicarious Trauma-Free Life, available at http://www.amazon.com/Victim-Advocates-Guide-Wellness-Trauma-Free/dp/150089706X.

Made in the USA
Charleston, SC
16 November 2016